Blood Transparencies

Blood Transparencies

Blood Transparencies

An Autobiography in Verse

By Randy White

Forward By Josh McKinney

BLUE OAK PRESS

ROCKLIN | CALIFORNIA

Published by Blue Oak Press
Rocklin | California | 95677
© 2016 by Randy White
Cover Design by Maxima Kuhn
Cover photograph, Black Forest by Roman Loranc
Interior Design by Kim R. Doughty
Author photograph by Patty White

Printed and bound by Bookmobile
Typeset in Palatino

Printed in the United States of America

Library of Congress Cataloging-in-Publication Data
White, Randy
Blood Transparencies : poems / by Randy White.

ISBN 978-0-9975040-0-2

For Mom & Dad

Table of Contents

Introduction

Before iPhones, before personal computers, before pocket calculators, before digital photography, before even digital watches, there were transparencies. Photographs shot on reversal film to produce a positive image on a transparent base, these transparencies or "slides" were mounted in a small cardboard frame and placed in a machine which projected the image into a screen or wall or, more often than not, a bed sheet tacked to a wall: "Each transparency was shot through / by a small still light, the kodachrome sediment / illumined, like the wall of an ancient cave . . ." (from "Blood Transparencies"). The process seems antiquated now, but to my generation the family slide show was a form of entertainment that rivaled television, and its prominence among the American middle class can be attributed to the social nature of a viewing. Family and friends gathered to see moments retrieved from the past, blown up and flung onto a backdrop where they were embellished with narration by the viewers. Naturally, agreements and disagreements ensued based on variances in recollection (That shot was taken in 1963. No, it was '64.) Call it the synchronizing of memory, a kind of twentieth-century myth making. The experience was, as Randy White eloquently states in the title poem to his moving new collection, *Blood Transparencies,* an attempt to "give substance to our past, for what was, / and how we lived it."

The photographic transparency is an apt metaphor for a poet with White's mastery of image. He understands the similarity between images both photographic and poetic. If the photographic image is a moment frozen, a "fossil of light / and darkness interned within celluloid," the poetic image is no less imprisoned. The temporal made spatial, both types of image are inexact, subject to multiple interpretations, multiple ways of seeing. It is the poet's job to interpret such images, to create stories to contextualize them, releasing them again into the flow of time. But as White observes in the poem "Woodland Stories," images overlap, blur, as the present moment, instant to instant, becomes the past:

I watch my mother iron in the picture window
of the rented house. Clean
white sheets snap in the breeze,
like pages in my storybook, slipping
past, to what I can only imagine.

Here the poet's recasting of memory in present tense further emphasizes
the ephemeral nature of the images. What we are left with, then, is a past
that only the imagination can resurrect.

Actual photographs appear throughout *Blood Transparencies,* embedded among poems that are not ekphrastic in any traditional sense as they
do not attempt to describe the photos. Rather, the photographs of White's
progenitors—parents, ancestors, the poet himself at various ages—provide
counterpoint; their images serve to catalyze the creative power of imagination. To the extent that a poem may elaborate on or provide a narrative
context to a photo, we are reminded once again that the photo is an image
originally torn from narrative, a moment of a life as it was lived.

Artistic creation, a re-membering, is essentially a quest for origin. Such
a quest demands an acknowledgement of blood in all its literal and metaphorical resonances. Like the many rivers that flow through White's poems,
blood is both source and route toward origins both personal and collective,
a tether to those who make us who we are: family ("Wrestling Odysseus,"
"Building His Kayak," "Homemade Soup"), neighbors and acquaintances
("T-Bone," "Mrs. J.," "St. Lucy Jones"), those lost in the bloodshed of war
("On Reading Homer," "Les Terribles"), and nameless others from the
archeological past ("Unearthed, The Taurokathapsia Fresco at Knossos,"
"Father Bones"). But White goes further still, tracing bloodlines back to an
animistic connection with other creatures, to childhood's early interactions
with the natural world and its non-human inhabitants. In "Wild Animals
We Have Known," the poem's speaker and his siblings, the children of a
game warden father, interact with a skunk kit, a bear cub, a raccoon—a menagerie that "accident, circumstance or arrest" have brought to their home:

We become brothers and sister, up poles
and down holes, chasing and stroking, licking
and biting each other, the world rubs off on us.
Apple dreams and sharp nails to draw sweet
blood and write blessing on our bare skin.

White understands that creative intelligence requires, indeed springs from, the ability to identify and to participate in otherness, while retaining a sense on one's own identity. As anthropologist Edith Cobb* has observed, "Childhood's willing acceptance and enjoyment of the muck and mire completes this power of creating mutual relations with the total environment and further empowers all levels of controlled thought in later life" (31). In "Tyee," "Our Sunday School," "Wearing the Bear" and numerous other poems throughout the collection, White's skillful manipulation of image renders articulate the child's wordless dialectic between self and world.

Again and again the poems in Randy White's new book reveal such mutual relations with the total environment. Family, friends, landscapes and fauna—all are characters that give substance to the past and how it was lived. A precise sequencing of discrete poems creates an overarching narrative of a life and the moments that shaped it. Above all, White is a story teller, and as our earliest ancestors were drawn to stories and sat bathed in the interplay of light and shadow on the walls of ancient caves, as our more recent forebears were drawn to the slide show, so too will readers be drawn to the luminous poems in Randy White's *Blood Transparencies*, poems that enact a timeless ceremony of creation as they wrest images from a past and reassemble them in the light of a master poet's imagination.

Joshua McKinney

*Cobb, Edith. *The Ecology of Imagination in Childhood*. Dallas: Spring Publications, 1993.

. . . innocence of eye has a quality of it's own. I
mean to see as a child sees, with freshness and
acknowledgement of the wonder; it also means
to see as an adult sees who has gone full circle
and once again sees as a child—with freshness
and an even deeper sense of wonder.

Lyric & Accurate, *Image,* Vol. 5, No. 8, 1956.
~ *Minor White*

Behind my eyes I carry a human education,
But the voices from without
Are incessant and overpower me:
The words issue up from the stones and the soil,
Sing in the river's current, whisper
Among the trees . . .

from The Man Who Hears Voices
~ *Bill Hotchkiss*

Definitions of Family

1. Taken from the Latin *familia,* family servants, domestics collectively, the servants in a household, thus estate property, an abstract noun formed from *famulus*: servant, slave.

2. Or later among the English, a collective body of persons who form one household under one head and under one domestic government.

3. Later still, persons related by blood.

A Perfect Fossil of Light

A Perfect Fossil of Light

Blood Transparencies

Sometimes after dinner
my father gathered the family,
tacked bed sheet to wall and gave a show:
The White Family Adventures!
His voice became Shakespearean,
inventing dialogue, creating a voice
to give substance to our past, for what was,
and how we had lived it.

Each transparency was shot through
by a small still light, the Kodachrome sediment
illumined, like the wall of an ancient cave,
like a red dirt furrow in an Oklahoma field
full of sunset, each frame centering
a moment, a perfect fossil of light
and darkness interned within celluloid.

We saw ourselves, set like beads on an eternal thread:
Wife with Fish, Daughters with Golden Trout,
Fresh Biscuits & Apricot Jam. Mountaintop with Son,
Family on the Summit of Mt. Whitney
at the End of an All-Summer Backpacking Trip.

And in that pause between slides,
that shutttle of darkness blooding the ceremony,
wings began to haunt, then batter themselves
against the bed-sheet-white geography,
drawn to the brief incandescence
of our lives.

On the Klamath River, 1953

Fishing the Klamath River, 1953

The father a fish, is the rumor among friends,
some great-finned river god up from the sea,
gone dark, losing his iridescence between her legs.
Downstream, an old Yurok dies laughing, mouth agape.

I float down spring's amniotic streams,
dreaming of the great blue branching,
watching blood stars fall in the darkness
the tide merciful beside her leviathan heart.

As my father prepares for summer, gills,
then the web between my toes disappear.
I listen to every promise ever made between lovers,
the vow never to leave as they were left.

But, even now, in the shade of my mother's breath,
angry blood knots in me,
as rising to the light,
water breaking, hands
like eagles come for me.

Why My Mother Wept When Edmund Hillary Climbed Mt. Everest

Saved in her dreams
that forbidden mountain, that glory
but more, the world knowing,
that honor upon her son.

Can you imagine
the light glancing off that white summit,
the whole world below
awaiting word?

But then, explorer, scientist,
any kind of hero would do.

What if I became a love-seat murderer,
or wore six-guns slung low, hitched up by baby fat.
What if I decided to kill blue singing creatures
or conquer all the known world?

What happens when I learn to make love?

Who could have imagined
stories hidden like camouflaged prey
in my veins: a faint blood trail
leading to a campfire
rather than down that mountain.

Tyee

I am the center of the universe.
All things move around me!
The black dog from Grandfather Hosmann
dances & sings about me.

I am the center of his world!
My shadow inside his,
I crawl, learning the world.
My parents name him Tyee, dog salmon.

Strangers come to see me,
hands smelling of bleach,
with gifts and blessings.
I prefer the pink heal-all tongue,
ass-sour in my face.

Black as an island, he sleeps
as I curl inside his dreams,
he bites off pieces of sky
to bury them, white as bone,
as seed in our future.

Building His Kayak

It rests, like the skeleton
of an animal I cannot name, my fingers
just fitting through wood ribs.
It smells of dreams: brine
and whitewater, dark broad seas,
the gap between Attu and Kiska,
bare lands with only stone boys
for companion.

Weeks later, I sneak back
and there is cloth wrapped around it,
taut as skin, a hole made in the middle,
room for a man and his gear,
or perhaps a man and a boy.

He paints it blue as a sky. What
are the words on its bow? What name
would swim like a fish across
the Bab-el Mandeb, a creature
made for wandering?

I fear water, and when I ask: "Daddy,
what is it that you are carrying on your shoulder?"
he only smiles.

Woodland Stories

Beyond this field at the end of the world,
where dark vegetable heads drink
furrows of still water all night, that
is where he lives, the monster.
That is the story an older boy tells me.

I watch mother iron in the picture window
of the rented house. Clean
white sheets snap in the breeze,
like the pages in my storybook, slipping
past, to what I can only imagine.
In the fields troll-shaped pumps
have turned to stone
for the moment.

Late at night curled on the sofa watching
The Tales of Wells Fargo, my mother
offers me a bite of her apple, my baby sister
screams, turning blue. I offer
to tell her a story.

Cowboy

Firsts

Picayune Valley, Sierra Nevada Mountains

Before I open my eyes
I hear the crack of kindling, blue smoky smell.

Sloshing around in an old Army/Navy mummy bag,
I wake in a piss-warm world
with mountains all around us.

Dad smiles and brings me a cup of "Don't-tell-your-mother" coffee.

The lake calms.
The universe begins.

The Redd

In the old beds of prehistoric trout,
in diggings, earth sluiced open by our ancestors,
we hide, throw wild oats that rain
down like Greek arrows, stick in us,
or shimmy up the forks of blue
oaks, squirreling away piles of quartz,
mistletoe, and cow pie.

Parents approach like old rivers come back,
bedding again through the hot gravel.
Leviathan fish, cannibals come to eat us,
their voices calling us home, like great mouths
feeding on unseen young
not even God can hide.

They will eat us with their lives,
if they can.

The Priest at St. Joseph's

We only sought God.

After all these years, she asks
for forgiveness,
to bless her marriage,
her three children.

But, to this Holy Father
we are bastards in the gray
eyes of God, unredeemable,
destined for Limbo.

I never heard my mother recite
another rosary. But watched
the words form at night
sinew through bone, not pearl
or when she feared for us,
breath bitter as incense.

Hail Mary full of grace
The Lord is with thee

What should I do
that evening
when I am father
my daughter
in her starched white
& blue-checkered pleats
recites the rosary,
asking where you will be,
Daddy, what happens
when you . . .

St. Lucy Jones

Instead of using the .410 shotgun,
or ball-peen hammer in a gunny sack,
my father hid under his car seat
we would drive up to Dutch Flat.

There a woman in a long polka-dotted dress lived,
where the lucky, the lost and the orphaned
fawns and other small creatures were offered up.

There among songs, whistles and cock crows
all creatures had free run of her world.
I chased her chickens through the always open door,
hopping as they scattered shit in terror.
Then out the back through the Kit-kit-dizze
Her old husband stood laughing
in those half-zipped, oil-stained coveralls.

She would warm milk and nurse
the hungry mouths, stroke
their wild energy
calm.

Her toothless smile reflected
in a milky puddle of dribble
on cracked linoleum.

Offers me a soda cracker
and calls me her little leper.

Blood And Blessings

Blood And Blessings

Wild Animals We Have Known

"Ask the beasts, and they will teach you."
  ~ *Job*

Four-legged trip-trap on wood, wings
flailing, spills, grrrr and crying
animals are brought to our house
because of accident, circumstance or arrest;
Dad is the Game Warden.

The skunk kit whose mother was run over
is nested among our new kittens, momma-cat
cleans him and our fingers, my sisters giggling.
A ringtail cat with eyes big as the black marbles we shoot at school.
A bear cub staked out on the front lawn
when we come home from school. Pelican
with fishhook in the pouch, lost fawns, bullfrog.
Bagila, the raccoon, curled, churling in my sisters' arms.

We become brothers and sisters, up poles
and down holes, chasing and stroking, licking
and biting each other, the wild rubs off on us.
Apple dreams and sharp nails to draw sweet
blood and write blessings on our bare skin.

War Games, October, 1962

The helicopter circles our house, settles
vulture-like, worn from chopping the blue air.
The sky congeals again over wild oats. Soldiers
cross the valley towards us,
avoiding our staked-out steer & cowpies,
their flight boots tangled in vetch.
Clean crew-cut boys drink my mother's coffee,
pick foxtails from their camouflage jumpsuits.
They are lost practicing war. They just want to call home.

Dinner is talk about where to dig the bomb shelter.
Andy and Opie and Aunt Bea are buried beneath the news.
We sit around the TV listening to the storm outside,
watching the black-and-white pictures shuffle
across the small screen.

Rain, blue oak leaves falling, mushroom clouds,
some dark opposite in our dreams.

Root beer made last summer explodes beneath the porch.

Mud Children

We dance a mud dance in the mud spot
stomped in the neat lawn near the curve
of our blue limestone driveway, near
the jungle of mother's purple rhododendrons
planted too close against the house.

Head to toes in mud, blue
sister-eyes blink back. Now,
we are like the people in the *National
Geographic* magazine
that live in little mud houses too.

I want to gather cow flops from the pasture
and mix it in, to make it as real as, but
my sisters scream and make a run
for Mother inside our big wood house.

That night black people are running
and yelling on TV. Houses burn.
Dad reminds us to be thankful,
to remember that there
are starving children in the world
who love creamed spinach.

Fisher Kids

Control Burn

His indifference is the trick horse left at the gate.
The Gray Tide turned back, this war begins with a burning heart.

My toy armies and heroes burned beyond recognition.
My imaginary kingdoms reduced to ash.
My father's god-like laughter.

I will never forgive Robert E. Lee, either.

On Reading Homer

Long after goodnight, house
dark as the belly of a ship,
I tent blankets to read his words
by flashlight, stories
older than writing.

My bed is an island, or some foreign shore
full of bitter love, iron in the teeth, or
the soft curve of waiting skin, dark wine
flowing, divine suffering, charmed silence,
a furrow where sleep is sacrificed to dream, words
seed fallen in blood, a variety of fate
in flesh cut by offered words.

I wake to tin ringing
on steel, to meat cooking
amid morning shouts,
my wounds beginning
to heal.

Les Terribles

For Harry Woodrow Larkins
32nd Infantry Division

He watches me strip leaves
from my mother's rhododendrons for ships.
Toy soldiers: Union blue and gray or jungle green,
charging across some field, or storm the beach,
on some imaginary Pacific island, my thrown rocks
spark leaving a smell like gunpowder,
the calm of a Saturday morning, until
the sprinklers begin.

He remembers,
the rain, zeros in the sky overhead,
the Girua River, palm fronds burning,
that 105mm named Helen
for the pretty brunette from Chicago,
the rain,
jungle ulcers, malaria, dengue fever,
dysentery, Waltzing Matilda,
the rain,
Japanese spiderholes, the shriek
of a .25 caliber, the fog lifting,
after rain.
After Buna and Finschafen, Leyte, Luzon,
after finding the POWs at Bilabab Prison,
after meat raining down into the cogon grass,
the heart in a ripped chest on Yamashita Ridge,
the rain.

He shakes his head
as I watch him walk away.

Wrestling Odysseus

"'Father, my wings are strong now, drop me from your claws!'
The ancient eagle shrieked with maniac rage and joy, beat his
enormous wings, opened his branch-thick feet and hurled his
young son headlong through star-burning air."
    ~ *The Odyssey, A Modern Sequel, Nikos Kazantzakis*

Sunday evenings after *Walt Disney Presents,*
my father teaches me how to wrestle.
My mother leaves the room, my sisters begin to cry.

This lesson I know:
half-nelson, full-nelson, headlock,
humility, rage.

This is my father grasping his father,
an old man, living alone by now.
I spit blood in the sink, explain away
the shoulder that never heals,
the delicate pattern
of rugknots in my cheek.

There is no honor, no prize of arms to win in this,
no lesson here but fury.

I do not understand

and I will not give.

Homemade Soup

At Grandpa's bar, whiskey-breathed old men
eat hard-boiled eggs and crack jokes I don't get.
Grandpa, bleary-eyed, drags out a few worn coins
to give me from a collection he used to have.
Remembering every memory sold for drink,
my mother is quiet all the way home.

Later, at home, I peer in the kitchen window
past her dead mother's tiny teacups,
her only inheritance.
I watch my mother miss her mother again,
and cut the eyes out of potatoes,
skinning them down to whiteness
before chopping off the celery heads
we gathered this morning.
Her hands beneath the water now
holding something down.

I want to draw on that steamed window between us.
I want to let what she might tell,
to let the unspoken weep.

Captain Jim White

Stealing Beauty

Shadow is milk where the roots go deep
like animals we dig each wild plant in turn,
begin a small spring at a wound that seeps
Black Bleeding-Hearts and Five-Fingered Ferns.

Like dead birds' feet from the side of a nest,
umbilical dark as the ball of a fist,
a mossed belly hole where the curve of a breast
will fill Mother's dream of a garden with mist.

Transported, transplanted in soil too sweet,
a beauty that burns in the full of the sun,
bodies gone dry, transparent as silk we beat
the bulbs free like a bouquet of small skulls.

My sister asks why blossoms snow, and
what do the leaves, these roots all know?

Our Sunday School

God is in the mountains
if anywhere, more
than some church,
my father taught us—

So we left messages
in empty sardine cans
under granite ledges
above small blue lakes
turning to meadow.

His sermons: pack light,
and where
to find good cold water.
why
break trail through spring snow,
and how
to catch rainbows enough
to feed the family.

Salty crackers and river water
were our communion.
Fire with song,
when
to choose
the unmarked route,
to prepare,
to flow from use
to use,
for the certainty
of becoming.

Feral Hearts

Feral Hearts

Variations on the Woolly Bugger

Isaiah 1:18:

"Come now, let us reason together, says the Lord:
though your sins are like scarlet,
they shall be white as snow;
though they are red like crimson,
they shall become like wool."

Begin with intent, trickery with the objective
of maiming, so twist the strawberry hair of your daughter,
strip sinew from the bones of your only son,
as you, named exactly letter by letter as your father,
were an only abandoned son,
around the tiny steel crucifix with a barbed hook,
wind the dark tinsel of your wife's dark dark hair again and again,
tight as a piano wire about a pinky before you resort
to the tiniest pair of scissors ever forged.

Set aside an evening to cradle your pregnant wife,
your shivering children,

as you hover forever at the end of a rolling cast
just above their wide open lives.

Great-Grandpa Classen, 1910

Our Garden

Asked to kiss her mother's death-blue lips. The body
of dark earth beneath her small bare feet. Ash
near the roots, olive stones between the garlic; crushed
pinecones about the strawberries. Her grandfather helps
till soil in a plot set aside for her, where together
they plant cockscomb, pearly everlasting,
and zinnias for a winter bouquet
for her grave.

~

Before all things, Mother asked Father
for garden space; and this year
our new house is built, within
earshot of their bedroom window
she measures a distance off, helps us
dig the wild grass under, before we claim
our plot of red dirt.

We dream of green rows and draw furrows
from one end to another of our realm,
tossing weed and rock towards the steer
staked in the unfenced pasture.
We plant radish and stick the empty
seed packet with the picture-perfect radishes
on a stick at the head of the rows.

She followed Grandpa Classen along rows of corn
past berries laced through a lattice of wire. Her task:
to place a metal plate across the ditch
to divert water old as the Euphrates
from one row to another; how sometimes
they traded vegetables for the eggs and milk they needed.

Littered with the unburied dead of my books, the garden
is a battlefield for bloody Greeks, cowboys
and Indians, The Blue and The Gray, hedgerows
of lettuce where red dirt clods explode, field gray
camouflaged in the pole beans. From the remains
of heroes radishes that burn in the mouth.

~

This year we move our garden west,
into better light, and start again.
Red rocks make a new wall
and Dad buys a second-hand rototiller.
We haul in chicken manure by the truckload
and Mom takes agriculture at the community college, reading:
The Principles of Field Crop Production and
the Western Fertilizer Handbook.

We dig holes through hardpan for fruit trees. Two kinds
of apple, a cherry, a plum and a peach. In the evenings
we ride a green-broke horse in figure-eights
through saplings till he bucks us off.

~

She said Grandpa Classen wore a red bandana like an outlaw
when he ground horseradish in the dirt-floored cellar
where the sauerkraut is kept in a white crock. When she cried
he gave her honeycomb from a wooden bucket.

This year we buy a hive of bees.

~

We bury our dead in the garden, sheep mainly, breech-lamb or old ewe.
One spring stray dogs ravaged the flock.

On the wall of her grandparents'
was a map of the old country, Helgoland, Holyland, red rock
jutted from blue North Sea. Barely room enough
for flowers or graveyards. When it rains here
the water mixes with the dirt and makes red pools like blood
where we make faces at each other. When the sun comes out
wasps and white butterflies carry away the red mud,
where we saw ourselves, to make nests.

~

Radishes big as a thumb and sweet.
Yellow squash sprawled down the mounds.
Tomatoes swollen with light, a black
and yellow spider weaves one green to another.
Artichoke gone to seed float away soft as wool.

~

She told us how her grandfather would touch
one flower with dust from another
then pull a soft bag over the blossoms
to keep the bees off, his pollinations pure.

My best friend's sister has corn-yellow hair,
and when I try to kiss her she runs away.

We go barefoot when we can,
turn the soil and pick up small stones
                           with our toes,
try to learn
                 all the stories,
remembering, the names of plants,
kneel eating berries
till our tongues turn blue
with slanders.

Mendelian Error

He lives on land claimed, stripped, sluiced out
a hundred years ago. Yet, the creek
still flows, eddies around boulders,
waiting for the return of salmon, humoring
the kingfisher with minnows.

Dad sometimes brings him a salmon, or venison roast.
Listens to stories of the old country.

On his shelves a German bible, Goethe and Schiller.
A book by Mendel: *Versuche über Pflanzenhybriden.*
He grows vegetables and flowers on a small plot,
keeps a hive. At night studies a trellis of stars
growing through the dark.

He never married, but sought bees and blossoms,
propagated for generations his flowers.
His life not worn down, but polished to this moment:
an impossible red, a red the color of flower that should not exist.

He saves the small black seeds in carefully folded envelopes,
as if they were a last letter, as if my sisters were his *kinder,*

> my mother
> as if
> she were daughter,
> or. . . .

> his life worn down to this.

The Salmon of Knowledge

This winter gift, given or taken, a gunny sack
of salmon from Nimbus Hatchery.
Each fish bearing a single wound
the belly, slit open, spawned out, empty.

We butcher them late into the night
on a gray Formica counter.
The lidless dark-iris eye like a wide-angle lens
includes its own dismemberment.
Old hacksaw blade saws the darkening
rainbow flesh into steaks, blood
thaws thick as honey.

Mother disguises salmon a dozen ways:
roasted, baked, broiled, poached, casseroled.
Cooked till the eyes pop out white,
tiny bones in the baby-pink flesh.

I sleep that night dreaming words made flesh,
swimming back upstream
in the baby-blue January darkness.

In my flesh I shall see God.

Later, creeping near my parents' bed their hands
stink and I can smell their cannibal breath.

Penelope's Remedy

"Callas absolutely refused to cry out as Carmen does
traditionally when she is stabbed and while the chorus
sings 'Toreador . . . l'amour t'attend!'"
> ~ *Jacques Bourgeois on a review of Maria Callas'*
> *performance of Carmen.*

Within the frame of our picture window,
against the blue of remembrance spread
to where the gray of oceans begins or ends, fashioning
strange islands of the dry hilltops where our father seems,
reclined in his armchair, libretto fallen, fixed
by her perfect siren's voice, spinning
from the turntable he built
during endless garage nights,
dreaming of what might of,
knots broken, pearls
scattering on the
green shore,
where clover
hums.

*Great-Grandpa Hosmann on
the Pomme de Terre River, Missouri*

Counted in Sheep Years

I

From our dreams, from feral hearts, with wild blue eyes
we painted you; our blood mixed with your blood
mixed with dirt, drying on dark cave walls.

Ten thousand years of caring, your bones
buried with our bones. Giving you honor, burning
your thighs wrapped in fat.

For generations my people led you across the river Aar
into the high meadows, Die Alpweiden, to sweeten your milk
on blue gentians. We sang to you all summer
until the French came and burned our village.
We ate grass that winter and died.

II

Mr. Blackford, the sheep rancher who lives beside Coon Creek,
gave us three lambs, from dead ewes, bummers he calls them.
Mom concocted a milk and we fed them from our old baby bottles.
We gave them names and giggled as they sucked
the fingers we fed them between slurps of formula.

That spring my sisters came home singing "Mary Had a Little Lamb."
They turned them loose and tried to dress them up,
collected their droppings in a tin can. We helped
put fat green rubberbands around their tails. Later
we found the wooly tails like snakes in the tall grass by the willow.

By spring, when we call their names they come running
to eat the treats we offer: old peppers, carrot tops, sweet corn silk.

~

A man came and sheared the wool off leaving bloody nicks.
My sisters cry, we play in the woolly piles till our hands soften.

My sisters baa and mix with this year's lambs, crawling
on all fours, Miss green knees and Miss brown knees,
grass in their mouths, playing in the pile of shear, hair
wild, full of straw and seeds, dandelion fluff.

~

At night the shearings fill with moonlight, and in their nakedness
the herd cries all night at their other mist-like selves.

~

They ate grass all summer.
We wore white uniforms to 4-H meetings.
Pledging our heads to clear thinking,
Our hearts to greater loyalty,
Our hands to larger service,
Our health to better living
For our club, our community,
our country, and our world.

~

At Christmas my father unwraps his new sheepskin vest.
Soft booties for my sisters, leg of lamb with green jelly,
pan drippings mixed with flour over bread.
We praise their sweet pink flesh and turn the ram in with the ewes.

III
We bury the stillborn, dog-killed, heart-broken animals.
They lay interred in the rocky soil.

This is our garden: tomatoes, corn and peppers,
roots reaching down to suckle where flesh
becomes soil that feeds the green that feeds us.

~

Tonight everyone has gone to town,
and the old ewe in the pasture has pleaded for hours.
It is her time. In the frozen grass, she stands
belly caved before hips, heaving nothing.

I remember the old words and reach inside her.
Heat and tiny hooves, a lamb shape I turn
so body follows head, before pulling, her pushing
the unseen comes loose, hitting the ground kicking,
the blood webbing my fingers back to fins.

~

For stillborns, we skin the small body, black baby wool
peeling like an orange rind. A bloody jacket for orphan to fool ewe.
They live in shed darkness, beginning to know one another.

~

Cornered by life, sometimes we become dumber, perhaps more angelic.
We sip broth off your bones when we are sick, or unsure,
trying to remember our lives before we were herded. You dream of
running, hooves sharp across steppes and mountains.

Mom tries to count how old we have grown in sheep years; and when
did my eyes change from blue to green to gray.

Hen Mothers

From the oak
Mr. Hancock's infuriate
cock-a-how
dare-you-doodle
shakes acorns
as my sisters
hurry his beloved
flock of one.

Tucked under
my sister's loving,
mud-freckled wing
something red
and white
polka-a-dot
pulled over
the patient cluck
of jungle orange.

The three hen mothers
squat in the yard
playing dollie-doddle-do
scratching for beetles,
bugs and seeds
as the sky
falls down.

On the John Muir Trail

Spilling Green

Spilling Green

Great-Grandma Cook

Says they tore his ears off, buried
and roasted him like a pig. Later,
gnawed like rats on his toes.
Before they gave back some parts,
a jawbone, a wedge of thigh,
to his sailors.

She likes to tell family stories . . .
brings out an old grass hula skirt,
dad in a little sailor suit, a neighbors poi dogs,
photographs of the house at Kaimuki.

So small, so thin, barely a breath,
I wondered if she really existed
except, like in the stories
she always offers us a cookie,
or candy hard enough to break teeth,
from a dish with the palm trees
and tiny tropical flowers.

My sister sleeps on the ride home
curled up like a puppy, suckling
dark sweetness from her fingers.
I dream I am a gingerbread man.

Father Bones

For Louis Leakey that evening in 1969,
just in from Olduvai Gorge, Kenya.

Arriving out of an earth
where bones wait to speak.
There is something elephantine,
fatherly in you
as we listen,
resting in your shade.

Before sunrise
the herd moves anthills
are kicked apart.

I drink from the flood.
My question lost in your songs.

Before Climbing Mt. Ritter

Wearing the Bear

For Uncle Lew Oliver & Aunt Win

My parents gone for the evening,
I slip beneath the felt, inside the black fur
& slowly rise, my heavy skull nodding.
I am bear!

Chasing my sisters through the house,
raiding the cookie jar, eating the Buttered Rum Mix,
sharpening my claws on living room furniture,
I grunt, slobber & fart loudly,
Master of the cave again!

My sisters will tell
but not tonight.

Dante's Children

We ride stingray bicycles, handlebars high
popping wheelies in the roadside gravel
on our way to the blue-gray state mental hospital.
It's the best show on this side of town.
On a Saturday afternoon, better than 25 cents' worth
of Three Stooges at the State Theater.

We laugh like crazy watching the patients
try to love each other, football helmets smacking
together, their animal grunts & shrieks.
Some wilt on sunny benches where the nurses
have set them like potted flowers.
Some I think have requested asylum from
those who became generals.
Some inmates see us
& call out the names of their dead children,
They claw their gowns open wanting to nurse us back.

I wonder in which room they kept my grandmother,
poured electricity into her blood, erasing with light
every song she knew.

Everyone is quiet riding home.

I Dream of Jeanie

We all want to get into her pants.

We sit on top of the monkey bars & tell dirty jokes.
A salesman is driving along and his car breaks down . . .
in a hundred variations.

We pair the new choir teacher with our music teacher.
(Though she doesn't like when my best friend & I
change the words to "Puff the Magic Dragon.")

I'm doing my state report on Oregon
& I love cutting the pictures out & pasting them down
& I used too much glue & the pages dry bumpy.
I'm reading *Wild Animals I Have Known* (again!)
and when I grow up I want to be an archeologist
like Heinrich Schliemann and discover Troy.

We all want to get into her pants.

Gerald, the new boy, & I argue about World War Two.
He and his brothers & sisters have blonde, almost white hair
& they speak German to each other when they think I'm not listening.
We all know their dad was one of Hitler's test-tube super babies
& fought in the SS because I heard my Mom whispering it to a neighbor.

My friends and I teach dumb third graders how to catch
a gopher and keep it in one's pocket all afternoon,
play marbles, beware of cooties, worship holy recess bell.

We all want to get into her pants
I want to get into her pants.

But what I can't figure out is how
both of us are going to fit.

Mrs. J.

She waits for us, as if perched on a strand of barbed wire.

From a country of strict rows where hard corn
was drilled into furrows on a flowerless plain,
where it may or may not have rained those years.

Like these chalk equations on her blackboard,
this teacher pins us to our desks with questions
she knows we cannot answer.

The brown girl beside me wears river canyon, black
butterflies hanging on tall purple flowers, her black,
hair, brush thickets just walked through.

Our answers are impaled, then suspended,
small translucent corpses, like glass beads her ancestors traded.
Sunday choir beginning . . .

We've seen the butcherbird display its morning's work,
                                    singing.

My sister Laura, atop Mt. Whitney,
after 27 days on the John Muir Trail

T-Bone

I invite the neighborhood tribe to our house.
Mr. Jones whistles for T-Bone our family steer,
pets him on the flank walks round
& shoots him straight between the eyes.
Slits the throat to bleed, eyes
rolling behind girly lashes.
Hydraulics whine as the meat hook lifts.
He sharpens his knife & smiles at us, tells
jokes as he pulls the inside out.
We're given the gut to drag down the pasture.
We kick it, calling ghosts, until it splits open
spilling green back to green. We learn
blood burns the grass greener.

Neighbors curse at my parents.

Later, I smell steak
from a barbecue down the road.

Unearthed, The Taurokathapsia
Fresco at Knossos

For my sister Kathy

We call this game bully.
I paw lawn with all fours
as my sisters tumble away
on giggling handstands,
maneuvering
to ride my monster.
Finally I charge,
fingers & ears transformed
into flying hooves & horns.
I toss, trample my
curly-haired baby sister
her small leg bones shriek
compounded, spiraling apart.

Light shatters
on unearthed stone
to reveal the monster's
shameful dimensions.

My sister Kathy on the John Muir Trail

Frog Music

"There is a mark, made on the soul in its first wrong doing,
    and that is a taint.
And the mark of that taint either widens or wanes
As the soul decrees in its inclination so will it be."
    ~ *William Everson*

Standing in the pond, tall as heaven,
I am a monster. Watching for frog music, squinting,
one-eyed against the sun, listening
for the soft yelps, squeaks and trills.
Then I hurl a rock among the chorus,
before spearing in the green shallows
those helpless swimmers, singers
of slimy verse. Even before gills appear,
their tiny hearts are impaled on my sharp willow.
Pink entrails flag & tremble, a silly wiggle
in my wake, so, in whose heart
does the colder blood course?

That night like so many others, I try to capture
Darkness in a glass jar. Hold the blackness, turning it
over & over like an odorous preserve,
a jelly thick as ancestral blood, fixing what I am,
this present, in the fallen light,
like the negative of an old photograph,
to see if my dreaming breath
is any purer a distillation of humanity
than my laughter at noon.

Words in the form
of Angels and Demons

of Angels and Demons
Words in the form

Everyone Mistakes Dad for
Marshall Matt Dillon

On stakeout with Dad tonight, he wears
spotless khaki, black holster leather
with Hoppe's No. 9 gun solvent.

We listen to the Southern Pacific trains
pull the summit and watch
for spotlights, poachers trying
to shoot deer out of season.

At midnight we unfold waxpaper
from sandwiches Mom made us,
drink hot chocolate from an old thermos,
and call coyotes with the siren
until they answer back.

Falling asleep to war stories: seaplanes
& green Navy beer, chipped beef
with gravy slopped on apple pie,
dreamy islands with strange names:
Philadelphia, Panama, Mindanao.

The Sulu Sea where snakes couple
in the phosphorescence.

Duck Hunting Near Tadoiko

In the cave of night we wait,
shivering in the flooded darkness.

As the world becomes, wings
pass overhead. We tremble,
call them and they answer,
descending over a thousand years,
in gyres appearing like magic, treading
air at the edge of this world.

Across the smooth walls of sky,
we draw with fire on the pale blue
morning shot with blood.

Abraham Schenck

Abraham's Hill

The old man, eyes rolling back, with a stutter
hires me with a handshake.

After school moving waterpipe from quince
to pear orchard. Next week

cherry picking, and a miner's inch of water, ditch
music, old as the Nile, hoed

down a red hill. Three kinds of plums to cull, trees
he and his father planted at my age

into land his father, landless in the old country,
left him. In summer, we pick

hard green pears for city people back east
and rest near a window, drinking

jugs of well water as his childless
wife teaches piano lessons for a few dollars.

Walking home the nighthawks begin to hunt
above the streams, my hands, older, red as dirt.

Accession Notes

For Mr. Cotter

In class, as in church, we learn Latin:
Coleoptera, Lepidoptera, Ephemeroptera,
like a chant, a form of magic.
We learn that painted on their wings
are the beginnings of the word.
Such words in the form of angels and demons
as monks made in holy books,
painted on animal skins scraped
smooth of muscle and hair;
Commentaries on the Apocalypse

We gather the tools of collecting:
net and Skippy peanut butter jar
with the blue lid like heaven
punched full of star like holes.

In meadows wings play above the flowers,
crowd a patch of mud, scatter
at a single word that's breathed.

In the woods under silvered bark
on black beetle shells,
a camouflage of wide-open eyes,
appetites chewing a secret
in the soft wood.

On a small mound
the torsos & legs of red
& black ants strewn
in defense of some queen.

Our teacher explains
that the idea of red was born
from the crush of eighty-thousand
cochineal bodies to color
the sleeve of a cardinal.

Deer Hunting

Long before dawn, cowboy coffee boils.
I catch up horses in the dark.
A last swallow before swinging up.
The slap of rifle into scabbard.

Through blue-mooned meadow
break ice crossing Wolf Creek,
we follow a drift fence to cut trail
up the mountain, stars still high,
the year's first snow still deep in places.
Finding & losing by moonlight
the old trail, sparks off steeled hooves.
The hobbled mules bell far below now.

Tie up before first light
cartridges rattle in my pocket.
We walk the ridge, moving silently,
no branch broken, no stone disturbed.

I lie in snow along the ridge's crest,
cold hours before a brown ear flickers,
antlers rise from the sage & sweet birch.
Breath tightens, fingers from glove,
slow pressure on the trigger
not unlike turning a page.

Lake Winnemucca Camp

A Room with a View

For Herb Jacobsen and the crew at Vaquero Camp

After the backhoe was through
and the hole dug down
to ancient river bottom,
we tilt the old crapper up
on broken fenceposts
and drag it down the hill a bit,
clear of the bunkhouse
and tackroom,
twist her south
toward the confluence
of two rivers
across a valley
spotted with cattle.

Hell! somebody said,
it's so pretty you won't even need a magazine.

The Fire's Season

The Fire's Season

Dedicated to the fire crew at Columbia Hill Station,
Nevada County, California.

"Young stranger, who are you?
I have not noticed you before in battle—"
~ Book Six, The Iliad

The First Season

Before I knew women, I knew fire.

Before I fought fire, I learned
where to find the burning, hand
poised as if in caress above black char,
after attempting to bury, or bathe away
the sudden heat, the flame left
inside limbs and stones
washed whiter than bone.

Saw fire, the purifier, flow through hills
hiding seed inside downed Ponderosa pine
or the mouth of an old oak stump. Felt
its hot bite, a mark left, clean as teeth
on flesh for days:
a good lesson.

Before I fought fire
I learned to breathe, learned how
to steady the blood, consider chaos,
hold and roll a word inside the moment
before deciding, before cutting earth
down to mineral soil,
charging in, or throwing lines
up the mountainside
smoke darkening
the words.

I heard from the Captain:
I wanna see fireline dirt the color of blood.
I learned: protect your buddies.

~

At night, I read in the cool pine barracks
of a faraway time & cities peopled
with dark women & dead heroes, cities in ash:
       Thebes, Tenedos, Arisbe.

Raised the stars & stripes every morning
before coffee hot & black.

Learned the only way to make a bed,
the Marine way, so tight at the corners,
a penny pops circles
back off the gray surplus blankets.

Ate C-rations & stale canteen water.
Learned 8 lbs. of water equals a gallon,
shoulders sagging under the weight
up a mountain of buckbrush
& manzanita at noon.

    ~

That summer, poured whiskey & beer
down a stray dog's throat
as three of us held him down,
& with pliers pulled the porcupine quills
from his muzzle.

Sat on the kitchen roof
& watched the fire at Purdon Crossing
wishing we were going.

In the evening, out of boredom,
calling coyotes with the truck's siren,
red light spinning . . . distant answers.

Wrote letters to a girl I knew.

Learned to use a chainsaw from an Arkansas redneck.
Cut a slice into the deadfall & wedge, backcut
& have the tree spin on some invisible axis
away to thunder.

Learned of strange war-sharp tools
named like some black forest heroes
Pulaski,
McLeod,
Single jack,
Brush hook,
Hazel hoe.

Up early to move stones from here to there
because we are here says the Captain.

Talked about women, dreamt about fire.
Sneaking off for a cold beer
from a neighbor's wife. Stretched out
under an old black oak.
Catching hell later.

Fella came up to find the waterline
taught us how to bend a coathanger
& witch for water dead on
the buried line, forks quivering,
pulling down.

~

Effie, the cook, asking if anyone
is unsure of who is the boss around the station.
Effie, The Old Crone,
Dakini-Of-The-Kitchen,
Devourer-Of-Young-Men
(the Chief's mother-in-law,
poor son of a bitch).

On her tongue blessings & curses,
ice-cool pitchers of Kool-Aid & milk.
Dish upon dish of weird stews & casseroles,
dark sweets & gingerbread men.

We called her bitch, witch, Old Hag.
We called her Mom (because she demands it).

~

Forever polishing those red & chrome fire engines: 2379 & 2361.
Had them shining like an apple for a teacher.

Did everything

but fight fire.

North Columbia,
middle of Bloomfield township, smack between
the middle & south forks of the Yuba River.

Holding down the fort, keeping to the big timber.

Ain't life a bitch!
That was our saying that summer.

The Second Season

Clouds like boxcars
starting up in the far mountains,
a small light, like incense
in the beginning.

Taper of pine,
manzanita candelabra,
dry grass,
a year's worth of newspaper,
everyone's garbage.

We memorize each scent
watch the smoke's color
guess the distance & size.
Listen to the wind,
trembling.

Dreamt of women, talked of fire.

Knew fire by many names
Canby,
Birchville,
Lake City.

Sat up all night listening on the station radio to the boys
down at Higgins Corners chase a guy who set 27 fires.
That crew beat the shit out of him before
they gave him to the cops.

And then fire,

Scotch broom burning like gasoline,
manzanita, hot enough to crack iron,
digger pines going up between us like matches.

Like I imagine rapture.

pitch crackling,
the pungence of tractored brush
as big yellow cats like tanks cut line.
One guy ran over a rattlesnake den,

snakes churned out rattling
as the treads turned up the red earth.

We wear khaki shirts & Frisco jeans,
red handkerchiefs around our necks
like a bunch of outlaws.

Ax in the knee, bush in the eye,
blisters blisters blisters. The beginnings
of stories and lies.

We listen to the names
of faraway places on the radio:
Hue,
Dak To,
Ben Tre,
watch boys burning
in insatiable fires on the evening news.

Little white scars
small . . . as the words
in a letter.

~

At two A.M., on a cold night in August, the last
building in Lake City gets torched.
This town once had a hotel,
a tailor shop and two saloons,
probably even a whore.

~

North on the Modoc fires.
Three days without sleep.
Steak & eggs for breakfast
iced quart cans of Del Monte grapefruit juice.

Bathe in the creek if you need to . . .
Everyone should but doesn't.

Jump out of a helicopter,

cut line through rock and watch fire
as it runs up the ridge all night,
flame in igneous stone.
Mind so alive after these hours
the eyes will not close.
We begin to lose our hearing
and hallucinate. Three of us lost
down some drainage.

Coming home
we swam in the Pit River,
piling our uniforms on bushes
and scrambled naked into the cold water
soaping up & don't give a damn.
Some local girls giggle and point from a bridge.

We all step in nettles on the way back to the truck.
Drive back to Redding, then home.

~

White horses loose
on a black hillside.
Six of our crew hurt
beside an old wooden schoolhouse.

Bombers overhead blades turning
in the darkening sky above red Nevada County soil.
Brown fire shadow, brown sun, cat-treads cutting
up the mountain, stitching the earth open
like a wound, a million years sliced open.

~

The Birchville dump is on fire again
& our engineer, Hawkeye, on two wheels again,
almost kills us against that oak at Peterson's Corner.
Grass snapping, eyes smart, noses running,
cough burning throats.

Birchville.
Nothing here.
but memories
& the dump.

Birchville burned down
in 1853
1865
1866 . . .

Effie
Steve
Mark
Ducky
Tony
Pete
Hawkeye,
The Captain,
that guy just back from 'Nam.

At the end of the season,
one to Sweden,
one a sheriff in Alabama
one back to his barrio in L.A.
One stayed
the rest scattered

. . . like seed.

Fireweed
Gooseberry
Poison Oak
Chamise
Manzanita
Ceanothus

. . . like sparks.

Hey White, are you ever gonna write about us?

The Third Season

Too many nights as a boy reading
under the bedcovers:

"All being gathered and assembled, first
they quenched the smoking pyre with tawny wine
wherever flames had licked their way, then friends
and brothers picked his white bones from the char
in sorrow, while the tears rolled down their cheeks."

has hurt my eyes,
culled me from the other fighters.

This season I will not fight fire,

but burn

wait like a meadow in anticipation as clouds build up
the moisture bluing as it swells above the mountains,
wind rising, seed heads shaking
before the thunder begins.

All the words I could say, yet
we hardly speak, only my breath across skin
the color I imagine the ancient deserts in Egypt to be.

Mystery burned away to sweet ash, memory
darkened by fire & her kissing the dry tinder
of my panic, kissing
my small white wounds with her lies.

I will know limbs sinuous as any manzanita,
thickets of elderberry afire, crude flutes blowing
a smoky song of renewal.

In the clean dark hills
the blooming passes through
as burning once did
seed time to seed time
one fire
called by infinite names.

Black Forest, Aspen Light

Black Forest, Aspen Light

The Reverend H.W. Cook

In the torn photograph, in his dark Sunday Preacher's suit,
with outsized left hand, he clutches a bible,
index nail poised at Revelations.

Is his right hand, gone from some war between good and evil,
or severed by some new machine of the age, or merely hidden?

We cannot hear the Mississippi at flood behind levees,
cannot hear snapping turtles the size of biblical shields
as they slide like dragons back from heaven to whence they came,
from whence we came. The world appears mended
for the moment by invisible hands, invisible motives.

We cannot hear the Quebecois in his sermons,
as he warned, of forests, a scribble of silver trees
poised above black water reflecting our troubled blood.

We can only forge stories from the mysteries, celebrate
our fall to paganism in worship of the trees and mountains
and rivers that lovingly break and bend and twist and break
and remake us a bit closer to

Snow Camping: Mother's Day

I remember through the perfect whiteness
of snow, of years, the long familial line:
my father breaking trail across the ridge.
Camp between lightening-stunted juniper
and cracked granite. Tent pole clack, stove guttering
in the cold, squaw wood snap, the slow-to-boil

soup from snowmelt as fire burns down.
My father's stories of John Hornby's last lonely
starving days, or Sir John Franklin's mistaken track
across the forever icepacks, a snow-blinded forever.

Dark peaks and unknowable stars, a last story
for snot-nosed kids with marshmallow fingers ends.
A last wet kiss burns, as sleep coils in mummy bags.
If words condensing out of hurt smear the unwritten page,
fire's embers, whisper and mouth forgiveness.

Grover Hot Springs

It stopped snowing just before dawn,
so we hid in alfalfa near a frozen lake,
under an old bed sheet invisible with flowers.
We waited for geese, the shotgun metal so cold
flesh stripped from your palm like moth wings,
if you let go.

Later, settling for jackrabbits, fixing a flat tire
in the sagebrush, we imagine warmth
as a friend tells me lies about his sister.

That night she joined us in a stolen snow cat, weaving
through a black forest churning snow up like fairy dust.
Then walking until steam rose up out of the ground, we climbed
the fence beside the NO TRESSPASSING sign.

She stripped first, diving shallow into the steaming water.
She watched us from the other side of the pool,
her brother winked and said: You should feel her titties - she likes it.
Shit, I said, you're her damn brother!
Man, she doesn't care.

We drink tequila and toast the New Year frozen three days old.
She smells like salt and sulfur, her white skin brown beneath the pollen
yellow water. I dive under and come up near her.
She takes my hand in hers twisting the tip of her long dark hair together
until it breaks off in my hand.

It begins snowing again, covering the dark limbs fallen
along the shore in light.

Basque Carving

In Aspen Light

For Joaquin, his father, and Uncle Domingo

Beside the river we find the old camp, ring
of black stones inside a grove of aspen. Around us
the trees are covered in carvings from generations
of Basque sheepherders.

Cuts become lines, on skin-like white bark turning black.
Likenesses exposed too long to light, or perhaps.

So many trees carved. Upon one a naked woman,
on another, the name for home, Euskadi, a man
holding himself, or a girl's name.

Here, two men are boxing, a couple holds hands,
a couple makes love surrounded by beasts.

A priest blesses a child. A list of years so long it winds down the trunk
like the memory of every lost home, or father, or discarded apple peel.

The body at burial should be like this, scarred, wound in song
our pitiful histories scratched on paper thin as light.

So many names. So many names for our loneliness.

Imagine their darkness filled with strange stars,
sheep crowded together full of sweet mountain grass.
The sound of one animal killing another in the night.

And when you waken, morning the same blue
as that above your village in another younger life.

Imagine their hands so soft from wool the knife
makes its own shape in their palms as they cut.

They were taught to cut and peel away the fleece, to expose
small sharp bones and muscle beneath, to wear the skin of the stillborn.

The tree coaxed to bleed and heal, to scar, to make over years
its own meaning from the wounding.

One shadow growing inside another.

Grandfather Ishi

Remembering . . .

after spelling words, catching gophers
in the schoolyard, and
the futility of long division,
we gathered in a circle around teacher,
listening to a story.

Thus I swam in my dream;
thus I could swim on,
coming at last to Outer Ocean.
Old Salmon could tell me
if the Lost Ones . . .

That night I dreamt too, swimming beside him,
grateful at his patience helping me
shape arrowheads from an old bottle,
learning to greet lizard and coyote,
in the sweet names of this new world,

siwin'i , yellow pine
?auna, fire
daati, child
dā'x, river
dā' si, salmon
dji-te' it, blood flows out
né 'duts! gil, he returned to the water

What is this other blood swimming in me,
this other ancestry made of dreams,
this long walk in a hard country?

I am trying to rebuild the fire Grandfather,
to see the journey clearly, jump through that hole
from this world to the next, climb into the sky,
so when we meet again beyond the Outer Ocean,
we can warm ourselves, share a coyote story.
So you will be proud Grandfather, so I can finally
speak your true name aloud again.

A Story

Notes to the Poems

Accession Notes: The detailed notes an entomologist makes when collecting an insect.

Attu and Kiska: Two of the many Aleutian Islands.

Bab-el-Mandeb: A narrow strait between Africa and the Arabian Peninsula that was a corridor for early human migration.

Basque: An ancient ethnic and culturally distinct population in northwestern Spain.

Butcherbird: another name for the Loggerhead Shrike *(Lanius ludovicianus)* who after hunting small birds or mice will impale them on thorns or barbed wire.

C-ration: a pre-prepared, individual, wet, combat meal.

Cochineal: An insect from which a red color is extracted.

Dakini: Sanskrit, "sky dancer," in Hinduism a female being of volatile temperament. An ancient priestess who carries the souls of the dead to the sky.

Helgoland: The ancestral home of one branch, Frisian, of my family.

Heinrich Schliemann: Controversial German archeologist who "discovered" the site of Troy, one of my childhood heroes.

Kaimuki: My father's neighborhood in Honolulu.

Kit-kit-dizze: an aromatic shrub in the Sierra Foothills of California.

Les Terribles: The nickname for a U. S. army unit fighting in the Pacific during WWII.

McLeod and Pulaski: Two essential hand tools for fighting fire.

Mendelian Error: An allele which could not have been received from either of its biological parents.

Redd: a salmon or trout's gravel nest in which its eggs are laid.

Ta'doiko: A Native Californian term for the Sutter Buttes.

The Salmon of Knowledge is borrowed from the Celtic tales of Fionn mac Cumhaill.

The Tales of Wells Fargo: A "western" television series

The Taurokathapsia Fresco at Knossos: This art depicts a bronze Age Cretan fertility ceremony, the taurokathapsia (purifying bull dance) where young men and woman ran at a bull, grasped its horns, and somersaulted over its back.

Tyee: a name for a male salmon.

Vaquero Camp: Literally, Spanish for "cowboy" camp. A former ranch outpost of the Dangberg Land and Cattle Co. of Nevada. The abandoned structures stand near the confluence of Silver King Creek and the East Fork of the Carson River.

Woolly Bugger: A popular fly-fishing pattern originating in England.

Yurok: an indigenous people of northwest California.

Notes to the Illustrations

These images were chosen to note my ancestral "family", based upon a recent DNA profile provided to me by the National Geographic Genographic Project.

Page 1: A Perfect Fossil of Light. Petroglyph of a fisherman on pahoehoe, just east of the pond, Kaupulehu, Hawaii.

Page 15: Blood and Blessings. Cultivating in the highlands of Sichuan from the *Shih ching* (Book of Songs), one of the oldest surviving Chinese texts, a collection of traditional ballads gathered about 600 B.C.

Page 29: Feral Hearts. Horse and salmon detail, probably promoting the concept of fertility, from a pottery shard found near Tiryns, Greece, circa 1400 B.C.

Page 47: Spilling Green. The "dance" of youthful Minoans somersaulting over the back of a charging bull, later in Spain known as, *the salto del testuz,* the leap along the bull's back.

Page 61: Words in the Form of Angels and Demons. First millennia B. C. "spirit" figures from Reboso de Nuestra Señora del Castillo, not far from the great cinnabar mines near Almadén, Spain.

Page 73: This archetypal symbol is found throughout both the Neolithic and modern world symbolizing fire, regeneration, water or air, and the Christian trinity.

Page 87: The Salmon of Knowledge, a Celtic design, based upon the story of Fionn mac Cumhaill in Irish mythology.

Acknowledgements

The author would like to thank the following: Bill Hotchkiss, publisher, poet, friend and mentor; poets Donald Finkel, Sharon Doubiago, Judith Shears, Eve West Bessier, Dennis Schmitz, Mary Mackey, and the late Walter Pavlich and Francisco X. Alarcón for advice and encouragement. Editing by Judy Crowe and cover design by Maxima Kahn. Thanks to Gretchen Franke, Rachel Holscher, Kim R. Doughty, and everyone at Bookmobile who guided this project. Molly Fisk for a keen aesthetic eye and joyous wisdom along the way. Carol Williams at Photography West Gallery in Carmel, California and a special thanks to photographer Roman Loranc for his photograph *Black Forest*. My love and appreciation for the support and patience of Patty, Elizabeth, and Jim White. This volume would not have been possible without the many hours of attention given to the original manuscript by an extraordinary poet, Josh McKinney.

Blue Oak Press Literature Series

The Blue Oak Literature Series embraces the breadth of culture, ethnicity and geography of the American West by publishing and promoting works by both new and established writers and poets.

Eileen Curtis	*Girl on a Mountain*
William Everson	*The mate-flight of eagles*
James B. Hall	*The Art and Craft of the Short Story*
Bill Hotchkiss	*Dionysian Chants from Woodpecker Ravine*
Bill Hotchkiss	*Fever in The Earth*
Bill Hotchkiss	*Jeffers*
Bill Hotchkiss	*Middle Fork Canyon*
Bill Hotchkiss	*The Graces of Fire and Other Poems*
Bill Hotchkiss	*To Christ, Dionysus, Odin*
Robinson Jeffers	*The women at Point Sur*
K'os Naahaabii	*Curios of K'os Naahaabii*
K'os Naahaabii	*Notes from the Center of the Earth*
K'os Naahaabii	*The Bitter Roots of Peace*
A. M. Petersen	*Stars in twilight and other poems*
Judith Shears	*New Leaves*
Edith Snow	*Hold Your Hands to the Earth*
Edith Snow	*The Water Mill*
Edith Snow	*The Good Yield*
Edith Snow	*Winter Tree*
Randy White	*Motherlode / La Veta Madre*

About the Author

Randy White is a writer and educator who lives with his wife and daughter in Rocklin, California.

Besides being the author of *Motherlode/La Veta Madre* (Blue Oak/Capra Press), he has been awarded the Bazzanella Literary Award for both poetry and short fiction. His work has appeared in the *Range of Light Anthology, From These Hills: Stories and Poems of The American West, Sulfur, Sierra Journal, Poetry Now, News From Native California* and other magazines. He was also a finalist in both New York's Inkwell Poetry Competition. A short story "In the Mouth of Heaven" was nominated to appear in the anthology: *Best New Voices in American Fiction.*

He gives readings of both poetry, fiction and biography and has appeared at Sierra College, The Western Literature Conferences, The University of Oklahoma, CSU Chico, The University of Arizona, Southern Oregon College and other venues as well as being sponsored to lecture on writing by Poets & Writers Inc.

Currently he is completing a biography of the Native Californian known as Ishi, and a young adult novel *River Sons and Daughters* about a boy who uses the power of story to save a river and his community from destruction.

Healing Song

I love the mountains.
I love the rolling hills.
I love the flowers.
I love the penstemon.
I love the fireside.
When all the lights are low.

Boom dee ah dah. Boom dee ah dah.
Boom dee ah dah. Boom dee ah dah.
Boom dee ah dah. Boom dee ah dah.
Boom dee ah dah. Boom dee ah dah.

I love the flowers.
I love the shooting stars.
I love the mountains.
I love the rolling hills.
I love the fireside.
When all the lights are low.

Boom dee ah dah. Boom dee ah dah.
Boom dee ah dah. Boom dee ah dah.
Boom dee ah dah. Boom dee ah dah.
Boom dee ah dah. Boom dee ah dah.

We walk together.
Hike by the quiet stream.
Watch for the sunrise.
Breath the air so clean.
When we're together,
sharing our deepest dreams.

Boom dee ah dah. Boom dee ah dah.
Boom dee ah dah. Boom dee ah dah.
Boom dee ah dah. Boom dee ah dah.
Boom dee ah dah. Boom dee ah dah.